Red Beans & Rice

RECIPES FOR LESBIAN HEALTH & WISDOM

Red Beans & Rice

RECIPES FOR LESBIAN HEALTH & WISDOM

by

Bode Noonan

illustration & design by

Diana Souza

THE CROSSING PRESS / Trumansburg, New York 14886

The Crossing Press Feminist Series

Cover design and illustration by Diana Souza
Text design and illustrations by Diana Souza
Typesetting by Marty Waters

Printed in the U.S.A.

Library of Congress Cataloging-in-Publication Data

Noonan, Bode.
  Red beans & rice.

  (The Crossing Press feminist series)
  1. Lesbianism--United States. I. Title.
II. Title: Red beans and rice. III. Series.
HQ75.6.U5N44 1986   306.7'663'0973   86-4175
ISBN 0-89594-195-3
ISBN 0-89594-194-5 (pbk.)

I *would like to dedicate this book to my mother, who part of me hopes will never, ever see it — not in a bookstore, not at the checkout counter at the supermarket, not at a friend's house, not even lying discarded in the gutter — but who another part of me wishes would find it and love it more than anything else in the world.*

Acknowledgments

I believe that people like you and me often share our brilliant ideas and deep personal beliefs only with each other. Too seldom do we make the connection with the ideas and beliefs that we all hold together as a congregation. Even less do we write them down in a form that can be passed down to the children who will follow us, or referred to during times of loss or confusion. Oh, we may exchange recipes scribbled hastily on found scraps of note paper, or phone numbers scrawled almost illegibly on the insides of matchbook covers dispensed in the bars. But who we really are? Sometimes we don't even give ourselves credit.

So I would like us to give credit to Laurie Hart, who has it in her to be one of the women who reaches the finish line of a Marathon race before any other person has crossed it. I would like us to give credit to Roxanne Layton, who simply, patiently and from a heart carrying sadness, explained to me the importance of human suffering one night when I was feeling sorry for myself.

I myself would like simply to acknowledge the existence of Ersy, Olivia, Janice, Betty, Manina, Stephanie, Jace, Carol, Tom, George, Ted, Susan, Jill, Dorothy, Charlene and Jim. I am so glad that they are in the world at the same time that I am in the world and that we know each other.

And finally, I love seeing my name on the cover as the author of this book. But you must know that this book embodies the vision and determination of three women: myself; Diana Souza, who insists that creativity be nurtured and shared; and Kate Dunn, who pulled the words out of me and now puts them out to you.

Contents

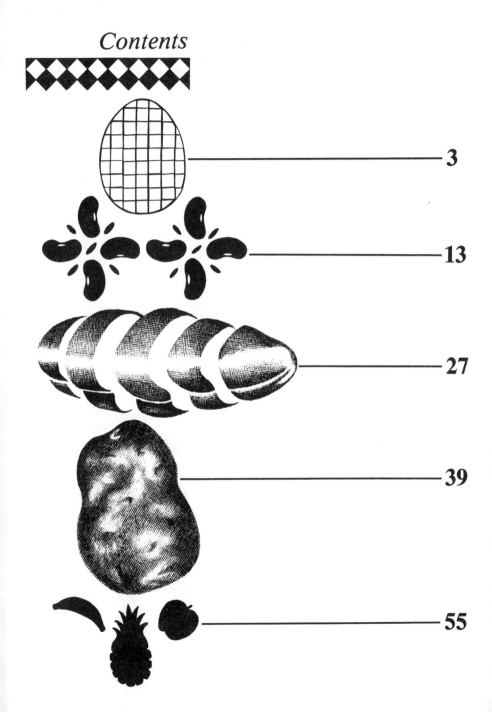

3

13

27

39

55

Egg
Salad

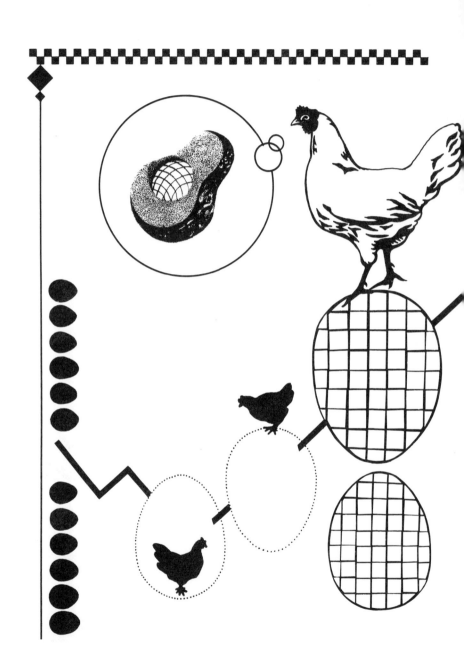

Okay now, egg salad is a wonderful thing. It's something our mothers used to cook for us, something they served in school cafeterias when they couldn't afford to put meat on the menu — remember those wonderful wimmin in the hairnets who we never saw as our own futures? — and something that is popular in health food restaurants today, at prices that make it seem as elegant as eating French cuisine in a New Orleans tourist trap.

And for those of us who are trying to get away from meat, giant supermarket chains, and working eight

hours a day for somebody else, I see egg salad as an alternative. It's cheap. It's available. It's nutritious. We're used to it. And we have to start somewhere; why not with egg salad? The secret here is in knowing what it is, learning how to prepare it, and being aware of where it comes from.

So what is it? An egg is almost a chicken. Which brings us to the question: should we be eating egg salad at all? I mean, is a fetus a human life? Is an egg yolk a living chicken? Should a womyn have an abortion? Does a mother hen grieve over the theft of her unborn chick? What if I eat something; does that give me the right to kill it? Is hunting for food a violation of the feminist code?

These issues are extremely complex and deserve careful personal consideration. I have a dream of living on a beach: taking morning walks, invigorating swims, and eating home grown grains, fruits and vegetables — communing with Nature and being at one with the Universe. But I live in Amerika and I am not wealthy. So I'm taking it step by step. And this step includes eggs.

So we have an egg yolk, which contains all the proteins, enzymes and minerals necessary to make a complete chicken; and an egg white, which is albumin — a simple amino acid chain. All this is protected by an egg shell, which we don't eat, but can give to our plants as a

mineral source. Now eggs are reputed by scientists — who are these people and why do they torture monkeys? — to contain cholesterol, a fatty acid chain found only in animal fats, which leaves horrible fatty residues around our hearts and inside our bloodstreams. The obvious solution here is moderation — we really don't need to eat as much as we do — and fasting, the body's natural cleanser. Also, the raw egg yolk contains all of the enzymes necessary for breaking down this cholesterol. Unfortunately, these enzymes, which are complex and delicate protein chains, are more easily destroyed by heat than the tenacious cholesterol chain. Probably the safest way to eat an egg is raw, uncooked, right out of the shell. But that is just too vile for me, and besides being no fun, would make a terribly runny egg salad — which brings us to the actual preparation of the egg salad itself.

When you fry an egg, you notice that the clear egg white begins to stiffen and whiten in color. This happens because the heat is fixing the amino acid chains into a particular spatial orientation. The more fixed they are, the less effective they are. In other words: heat isn't the greatest thing in the world for protein. So when you boil your eggs for your egg salad, try to cook them as gently as possible. I don't think you need to boil them in spring water, unless of course, you are the type of per-

son who mops your floor with spring water. Actually, I let cold water run into the pot with the eggs before I peel them, and then peel them right there in the cool water. So it's not a bad idea to at least rinse the peeled eggs in spring water after all. I mean, why eat any poison at all if you don't have to?

At any rate, do boil your eggs over a low fire. As soon as the water begins to boil, turn off the flame and let the eggs sit covered in the steaming water for about ten minutes. It takes practice to figure out exactly how long to cook them, but basically, you want your egg yolks to come out somewhere between hard and powdery, and liquid; and your egg whites soft but not runny. My perception of my mother is that she puts her eggs into a pot of water, turns the fire up high, and lets them cook, cook, cook for no less than twenty minutes. I think she thinks she's making basketballs. Then she chops them up real fine with one of those dime store food choppers where you hit the top of it repeatedly with the heel of your hand so that it pushes metal blades really hard onto the pulverized basketballs. Me, I'd rather use a knife and fork and cut the eggs lovingly into chunks. It seems to taste better, and is much easier on the emotions.

What kind of mayonnaise do you want to add to your carefully prepared eggs? There are the commercial mayonnaises that you buy in grocery stores, and the health

food mayonnaises that you buy in health food stores. Here are examples of each of them. One is Hellmann's Real Mayonnaise, which, according to the label, contains soybean oil, whole eggs, vinegar, water, egg yolks, salt, sugar, lemon juice and natural flavors and calcium disodium EDTA added to protect flavor. The other is Hain Safflower Mayonnaise made with, again, according to the label, 100% safflower oil, fresh eggs, cider vinegar, natural honey, salt, lemon juice and natural seasonings. What are these natural seasonings and do they include plastic? Fortunately, neither of these mayonnaises claims to use MSG, monosodium glutamate, a vile substance that makes you swell up and itch for the sake of flavor. So what is the difference here? Well, the most obvious to me is that the Hellmann's costs $1.66 for a 32 ounce jar, or slightly over 5¢ an ounce; while Hain has the audacity to charge $1.18 for an 11 ounce jar — at almost 11¢ an ounce, more than twice the price of the more commercial brand. Oh, I suppose they have an explanation, but explanations don't pay my rent. Nevertheless, there is a difference in health and quality here. Safflower oil is one of the least, if not the least hydrogenated of all the vegetable oils. The carbon chains that make up hydrogenated oils are much more saturated with hydrogen atoms than those that make up unsaturated oils, like safflower oil. The

hydrogen atoms in unsaturated oils are replaced by double bonds between the carbon atoms that make up the chain. These double bonds strengthen the chain so that it remains a liquid at lower temperatures than the hydrogenated oils. Consequently, the Hain isn't as apt to get as hard in our bloodstreams and around our hearts — like for instance, Crisco — as is the Hellmann's. Personally, I don't think the difference in saturation between safflower oil and soybean oil is enough to warrant a 100% difference in price. Of course the Hain Mayonnaise is better; but is it worth it? Maybe if we all bought Hain Mayonnaise, they could produce more for less. Actually, I have entertained the idea of making mayonnaise and selling it to my friends. Or you could make your own mayonnaise and sell it to me. Or whoever has the time and the inclination could make a big batch and sell it to the entire local Lesbian community. But I digress. Back to the egg.

Where do eggs come from? Chickens, of course. And how these chickens are treated determines how life-giving their eggs are going to be. We've all heard the horror stories of how our non-human sisters are treated — living in cages so that their claws grow around the wires and their vaginas turn to grizzle. Buy your eggs from a Farmers' Market where you can talk to the

farmer about how he or she treats his or her livestock. Establish direct communication. Visit the farm. Buy a chicken. I remember when I was a little girl, my father brought home six tiny chickens all dyed different colors for Easter. My mother was aghast because she knew who would have to take care of the little monsters and bury them when they expired, hopefully in a couple of days. Well, they didn't expire, and my dad and I built a coop in the backyard. And soon we had six big chickens who laid eggs and made a lot of noise in the morning. I was a little disappointed that they didn't grow up pink and green and blue like they were when my father brought them home, but I loved them just the same. I loved them and we had eggs until a cat got into the coop and bit them on their necks. I loved my father too, until cancer took his body. I love him still, but that's a whole nother story.

If we can raise our own hens, or buy eggs from Lesbian wimmin who raise their own hens, and mix them with mayonnaise that we make ourselves, we are one step closer to freedom. I generally add a scant teaspoon of Zatarain's Creole Mustard to my egg salad, because the world is full of many things and I want to taste them all. I never add salt because any more than is already in the mayonnaise is poison. Put a generous dollop of Les-

bian Egg Salad into half of a fresh avocado and top with a sprinkle of diced, spring water rinsed tomato. Think about Heaven and bring it home.

Red
Beans
&
Rice

Red beans and rice. Mmm good. New Orleans. And you don't even have to shoot them to get them into the pot. Or knife them, or chase them with clubs or psychologically motivate them to give up their lives for the cause of humyn hunger. They're totally helpless. All you have to do is rip them out of their warm, dry little pods, where they've been swinging from their safe little stems, thinking their little bean thoughts and doing their little bean things, and boil them in water until they die. Murderers! Electric chair for all farmers! Killing, perpetrated by men for men. Kill men! Stop the

indiscriminate killing of beans! But then what? What do we live on? Air, water and sunshine? We'd die. There are certain basic compromises one just has to make to exist on this planet. And one of them is that because beans seem to have no feelings, it's all right to kill them and eat them. Face it; it's either them or us. And what would the world be without the humyn race? Nothing but huge plants, expanses of gently rustling wheat fields, soft breezes, still water, mystifying quiet. We just have to be here! Or do we? Well you just can't think that far or you'll never get anything done. We are here and we just have to accept it and get down to the serious business of what beans are, how to cook them, how to eat them, and what to do about the gas.

So we have white beans, red beans, pinto beans, lima beans, mung beans, soy beans, has beens — No, no! Has beens. That's too silly — garbanzo beans, lentils, peanuts, split peas. And all these things are known as legumes. Oh fine, you say, that tells me a lot. What the hell is a legume? Some type of bicycle? No, a legume is actually a type of fruit. A vegetable is basically a plant that you eat — like turnip greens, broccoli or spinach. You just pull it out of the ground, wash it, cook it — or not — and eat it. You can eat the leaves, you can eat the stems. You can eat the roots, you can eat the stems and the roots. You can eat the buds. The whole plant is up

for grabs. But a fruit — which is also a plant that you eat and can therefore, by definition, also be a vegetable — is a little different. With fruit, you don't eat the whole plant. You eat the fruit of the plant. All fruits arise from flowers and therefore are found only in the flowering plants. When a plant flowers, the ovary inside the flower develops and matures into what we call a fruit, which then produces seeds. From these seeds, a new plant grows, flowers, bears fruit and produces seeds from which a new plant grows, flowers, bears fruit, produces seeds and so on ad infinitum as long as we are here — or not — growing food. Take for instance the apple. You don't eat the apple tree as if it were a vegetable. You eat the apple. You eat the fruit of the plant. Sort of like eating a mother's little children. Oh stop it! Right now, this instant! Just think of the fruit of the plant as the seed and its surrounding parental tissue. Okay, now here comes the legume part. With legumes, the surrounding parental tissue, instead of being soft, pulpy and delicious like it is in the apple, consists of a hard dry pod. And the seed — the seed — is the part that you cook — or not — and eat! Now on to the wonderfulness of meatless red beans and rice.

The beauty of this beans and rice thing is that because of the nature of protein, you can leave out the meat and still have a good, hot, nutritious meal. Of course,

nobody does. It seems to be second nature. You go into a restaurant, order red beans and rice, and what do you get? You get red beans and rice and ham. Red beans and rice and pickled pork. Red beans and rice and sausage. Wouldn't it be nice to have a lighter alternative? Red beans and rice. Period. Even my mother — you really didn't think I could get through a whole meal without mentioning my mother, now did you? Even my mother is subject to this meat delusion. Her words to me when she gave me her red beans and rice recipe were, "Now Babes (she calls me Babes), first thing you do is get a pound and a half of pickled pork and a little ham to make it good." What can I say? "Mom (I call her Mom), I'm a Lesbian and I believe wimmin can throw off this yoke of submission and dependency that you spent most of your life preparing me for. Thanks for wanting to protect me from the hardships of your reality. But I can still remember being a little girl and being free. And I want to be free for the rest of my life. I want to eat beans without meat." No, I don't say that. Not so fast anyway. Quite settled in her ways now, my mom has a hard enough time understanding me, much less the nature of protein.

So what is this protein anyway? Well for starters, proteins are huge, complex molecules which account for most of the body's cell structure. Proteins can be considered the building blocks of the body, contributing to the growth of muscle, blood, skin, hair and internal organs. They are composed of carbon, hydrogen, oxygen and nitrogen — the stuff that we are. These elements are arranged as amino acids, which consist of an amino radical and a carboxyl radical, both attached to the same carbon atom. Sort of like some of your more demanding Lesbian relationships. There are about twenty-two of these amino acids, and the spectacular thing about them is that the carboxyl radical of one reacts with the amino radical of the other to form by condensation what is called a peptide bond. So we can actually picture the protein molecule as a long, coiled or spiraled chain of some five hundred or so amino acids arranged in various combinations and joined from front to back by peptide bonds. Sort of like the wild tales of back rooms in men only leather bars on Mardi Gras nights. Whew! Nothing like a little male sexuality to jolt the Lesbian sensibility! Now that I have your attention back, the body produces all but eight of these amino acids, which we have to find and eat to stay alive. These eight amino acids are referred to as essential amino acids, and their names are Tryptophan, Leucine, Lysine, Methionine, Phenylalanine, Isoleucine, Valine and Threonine. Remember that the next time your dog has a litter of puppies.

There are complete proteins like meat, cheese and eggs, which contain all eight of the essential amino acids in the proportions that the humyn body requires them; and incomplete proteins, like some vegetables, legumes and grains, which contain only some, or are low in some of the essential amino acids. So a secret of good nutrition lies here in the combination of complete and incomplete protein foods so that the body's amino acid requirements are met. Then there's the concept of the limiting amino acid. We eat these proteins that we find in food and break them down into their individual amino acid units so that we can reassemble them into the proteins that we need. And there's always one little bugger that's either missing or in short supply. And that little bugger is known in scientific circles, where they cage dogs and don't give them any water and then try to figure out why they die, as the limiting amino acid. When you run out of that limiting amino acid, the body cannot produce a protein that it may need if that particular protein requires the missing amino acid. In that case, though the body continues to produce proteins out of the amino acids it has available, a necessary protein requirement will be left unfilled. Since the body cannot store amino acids, the excess amino acids are broken down and eliminated. What I am saying here is that you can eat tons of protein and still suffer from malnutrition

or disease if your diet is missing or deficient in just one of the essential amino acids. Now beans and rice eaten separately are fairly low sources of protein. Eaten together however, the two become a much better source of protein. Rice, though it is deficient in Lysine and Threonine, can compensate for the deficiency of Tryptophan in beans. Beans, though deficient in Tryptophan, are a very good source of Lysine and Threonine. Voila! Balanced meal. Warning: It is not as easy to execute this combination technique with relationships.

It seems that often when I cook a pot of beans, I forget just how I did it the time before. I lose my confidence and figure that it's all too abstract anyway so I may as well just hang it up and do something a little more predictable. Like Mrs. Drake sandwiches or Tastee Donuts. But then I have the beans and I have the pot and I really do like red beans and rice, so why not? The main imperative here is spring water. No matter that you may drink polluted city water all the day long. Once you've tasted beans that have been cooked in spring water, you'd rather cook them in Coca-Cola or Heineken Light than spoil them with that chemical taste. First thing I do is rinse and sort a one pound bag of beans. I take out the rocks and twigs and wash off the dirt. I have a good pot. I asked for one for Christmas one year. It's a Magna-Lite Dutch Oven. I like it. So I

put the beans into the pot, add six cups of spring water and place it uncovered over a high fire. While the beans are starting to cook, I chop up a medium onion, two or three toes of garlic and put them into the pot along with about an inch of a stick of butter, two cupped palmfuls of salt and a few dashes of pepper. By this time, I'm ready to turn down the fire, cover the beans and look around the kitchen for whatever else I can add to this soon to be sumptuous repast. Bayleaf, bell pepper, celery, parsley, mushrooms. Mushrooms. I remember how pleased with myself I was the first time I added mushrooms to my beans. They added just the right consistency that I had lost by taking out the meat. A sprinkle of basil. A pinch of thyme. A pair of old shoes and a felt tipped pen. No, no. Not a pair of shoes and a felt tipped pen. One must use a little judgement here. Still the possibilities of various taste combinations are many. And the dynamic of cooking always turns out to be the same. Covered, over a low fire, careful to see that not too much steam escapes and not too much water boils over, the beans seem to want to cook for about an hour before they demand another cup or so of water. Another fifteen minutes, and a few of the beans will lend themselves to being mashed against the side of the pot to thicken the whole concoction. A taste, another fifteen minutes, and they're done. And I'm always

amazed that me and the little beans have done it again.

But all is not perfect with red beans and rice, I'm afraid. One time I cooked a red beans and rice dinner for some new friends and was met with the devastating announcement, only an hour after the meal, that my primary relationship, as I had known it for seven years, had come to an end. My lover had found one of the dinner participants attractive enough to replace me in her heart and exclude me from their relationship. Not merely a casual flirtation, this attraction would change the way we were to perceive each other in a world not overly supportive to Lesbians. In searching for new ways to relate to new people, out of a couple, strong in my own independence, I lost the one aspect of my life that alone I would have chosen to keep. And so it goes with beans. We are seduced by the lack of expense, the promise of satisfying taste sensations and the prospect of company for dinner. And what is our reward? The turbulence and burbulence of intestinal flatulence. Flatulence is the result of the action of putrefactive bacteria on non-absorbable sugars present to a certain degree in all legumes. However, this natural flatulence can be kept to a minimum if one controls one's posture, the amount of air one swallows, and the amount of pantothenic acid in the diet. By eating beans without meat, the amount of intestinal putrefaction is greatly lessened. Taking a walk

after eating will stimulate gut motility, preventing the buildup of foul pockets of gas. I guess we can take care of ourselves. Simple, natural and politically correct solutions to the problem of Lesbian Gas.

I remember my first Lesbian love, and I don't mean my first crush on a camp counselor when I was seven, or my utter devotion to my gym teacher when I was in Junior High. I'm talking about being seventeen, sexual and in love. I felt like I was the only person in the world who felt love the way I did. That the woman I adored wanted to return my love was a gift from the heavens, for which I was to be eternally grateful. I wasn't going to spend my life alone. I had found someone like me, who not only wanted to be with me, but loved me as much as I loved her. Now we are adults, working together as a community to create a world where the Lesbian sensibility is given equal tolerance. Tolerance indeed! Where the Lesbian sensibility reigns supreme! At least we are out. We can dance together in our own bars, dismal though they may be. We aren't forced into roles. We don't get arrested for wearing pants that zip up the front. We are opening up the world for ourselves. We are fighting the fight for freedom. But every once in a while, we seem to slip back into those anguished days of adolescent loneliness, suffering an emptiness whose only relief seems to come from the promise and fulfillment

of new passion. Emotions are tried. Friendships suffer. Trusts feel betrayed. A community becomes divided. We don't need to eat every plate of red beans and rice, delicious though it may appear, that is placed in front of us. If our systems don't feel ready to digest a potentially flatulent meal, well, we can always eat something else. The kitchen is full. At least it's more full than it was ten years ago. And if we work together, we can stock it so high that we won't have to resort to losing ourselves in each other's lovers as our most fulfilling form of group entertainment. We can dine like queens. So please pass the hot sauce and cut me an extra slice of French bread, cause I'm hungrier than I've ever been before.

Bread

I'll bet you think I'm going to write about bread. What it is, how to bake it. Where to buy it, how to eat it. Should we eat it, can we kill it? Well, surprise. I'm writing about spinach.

Why the deception, you ask. Why say bread when you mean spinach? Why say unmarried woman when you mean radical lesbian? Why say lesbian when you mean dyke?

I'll tell you why. Because the truth is hard to take. When you serve a spinach casserole that is one bunch of spinach cooked with four slices of soaked, stale French

bread, there's no getting around the fact that you're eating bread, not vegetables. You're eating bread so nobody goes to bed hungry. You're saying unmarried because dyke means you might get punched in the mouth. Dyke means you might not get the apartment you want or the job you need. You might not get the money you deserve to buy the bread you need to pretend you're eating the vegetables you want to stay alive. Dyke means being sneered at by your straight sisters in public restrooms and college dormitories. Even worse than that, dyke means your own mother, your source of life and nurturance, might reject you.

So what I'm writing about here is not bread, though I will write about bread. Or even about spinach, though I will write about spinach. But about love and dependency. Mothers and daughters. And the survival technique of denying the truth. Denying the pain, injustice and actual fear that is living, and living defiantly, as women without men.

So why am I so defiant? Why can't some man tell me hello on the street without me wanting to kick his head under a public service bus? Why do I idolize my father and blame everything on my mother?

That's what Freud says, you know. You bleed through a little hole where your penis should have been, and your mother made you crazy. Boy or girl, it doesn't

matter. Your mother made you crazy.

I love my mother.

Never mind that your mother may have been crazy herself.

I hate my mother.

Or her mother before her.

I am my mother.

And my mother is special. But somewhere along the line I think she got tired of being special and getting nowhere with it. So she decided to have herself a special little child. A child whose special little hopes and dreams would not be dashed and shattered on the cold hard pavement of reality, but would be nurtured and protected by her own special sharing of her own special experience.

So she married my father.

And right there, right there, whether she knew it or not, I think she bought into a system in which she didn't fully believe. I think she spent the rest of her life cleaning her house and criticizing my father in a vain attempt to erase all traces of him and what compromise their marriage meant to her. I think she cleaned and ordered and nagged and denied herself into such unhappiness that she turned her sharing into control, her love into possession and her brilliance into cruelty.

"We're supposed to be miserable and sad," she told

me one day. "God wants us to be miserable and sad."

And I am sad. I am lost. I am in prison. I feel a heaviness in my chest and arms and a desperation in my head. And there are few things I can reach out to to know that I am real.

My blood.

When I feel that I am dying and can take this life no longer, I want to cut my body to bring me back.

When my mind is spinning and I feel an electric trembling surging through me like a current; when I am destroying physical manifestations of my self in the world and lashing out with horrible vindictiveness and accusations against those I love the most; when I realize I have gone too far or can go no further without going too far, I want to grab whatever broken glass, knife, razor blade, sharp edge I can find and determinedly slice the flesh of my wrist, arm, neck . . .

No. Not my neck. I don't want to die.

I only want to bring myself back.

Back from the giving in to what I see as my dissatisfaction with the injustices life seems to have dealt me.

Back from the total giving in to my anger at being mistreated as a woman.

Back from my rage, my intolerable rage, against oppression.

I am breaking out of prison.

And my blood brings me back.

Back to the world. Back to my existence. Back to my mother. My mother who cooked for me when I was too small to know what cooking was. My mother who gave me food from her breast when being two people was still new to us. My mother who I blame when things go wrong because she is the first thing I knew.

My mother who lashed out at me when she too could take it no longer.

I talked to my mother the other day. About her spinach recipe. I talked to my aunt. My godmother too. Hoping, in the back of my mind, to find some sort of revelation about the human condition. Maybe just a closeness coming from the admission of a common bond. Not just a bond of family, but a bond of sisterhood. A feeling of being women in the world.

"What gave you the idea to put bread in spinach?" I asked my mother.

"I don't know. That's the way my mother always did it," she answered.

"Why do you think Grandma put bread in her spinach?"

"Well, we didn't like spinach. We'd eat it if she mixed it with a little bread, a little butter, a little egg, a little onion."

"The bread holds the spinach together," my god-

mother added.

"Well, do you think Grandma's mama made it up?"

"I know they used to use rice for stuffing. I don't know what made them decide to use bread. I guess they just had it around."

I guess what I wanted them to say was that, as women, they'd had a hard time fighting oppression in the world, and put bread in spinach when times were lean to keep from giving in to The Man. I had an image of a kitchen full of wimmin gathered around a steaming pot of Revolutionary Gruel, bayonets at the window, poised to ward off the evil men who would wantonly rape, pillage and take hostage. I saw drums, bugles, blood-soaked bandages and patriotic flags. One womyn stumbling, another rallying behind her to take her place in the defense of her nation. Her Lesbian Nation! Full speed ahead! Damn the torpedoes and please pass the bread!

Needless to say, my expectations were not met.

But what I did see in my conversations with the women of my family was a great persistance, a strength; a passing down of heritage, survival. A deep belief in a Christian God. And with that belief, a stubborn refusal to even consider that their lives may have been influenced by male domination.

"Oh that Women's Liberation," they say.

Yet I sensed an undercurrent of resentment.

Do you know that until 1953, when a woman challenged the law, a woman teacher in Louisiana was automatically fired if she got married?

I sensed a fierce pride.

When my great-grandmother Elizabeth's husband died, she and her four small children moved in with her mother Barbara, whose husband was already dead, and Barbara's two sisters. My godmother, whose mother was one of the four small children, told me with a swell in her chest and a gleam in her eye, that Barbara supported them all by taking in sewing for fifty cents a day and that they always had wine with their meals.

I sensed a budding awareness coming to them with age, and with the increasing distance from the years in which they made the decisions that shaped their lives.

My mother says that she always thought she was eating bread and butter and salt and pepper sandwiches because she liked them. She says she never realized she was eating them because she was poor.

And who was to tell her differently?

Certainly not her mother who, with love or aggravation, fixed her those sandwiches.

Who is to tell her that there has been a war and we have lost it?

Who is to sit down with the flesh of her flesh and tell

her that the cards are stacked against her? That her options are submission, selflessness and childbearing? And that the consequence of rebellion is exile?

Not even her daughter, whose confrontations bring with them mutual accusations of failure.

And so we women are kept isolated from each other. In order to hold on to the few crumbs that are tossed our way, we deny our shared experience of womanhood; and in so doing, we deny our selves. And the very few that get a chance at the whole loaf do so in exchange for their allegiance to a system that keeps them on a tightrope and holds their sisters, their mothers, their daughters down.

And we call this survival.

And sometimes we call it love.

This loving protection, this sparring that sends us crippled into the world, dependent upon whomever would grant us asylum.

And so I will tell you what my mother has told me.

You cook two packages of frozen chopped spinach in salted water and drain. Sauté a medium onion in a stick of butter in a medium sized saucepan until golden. Soak about four large slices of stale French bread in a bowl of water. Add the cooked spinach to the saucepan with the onion and the butter and stir. Squeeze the water out of the French bread and break it into small pieces in the

saucepan. Add one raw egg and quickly stir everything together before the egg begins to whiten. Salt and pepper to taste. Cover and cook over a medium heat until dry, stirring occasionally. Put in a casserole dish and decorate the top with hard boiled egg slices. Serves the family.

And now I will tell you what she hasn't told me.

Though I have wanted to be my father's, I am my mother's daughter.

Potato
Salad

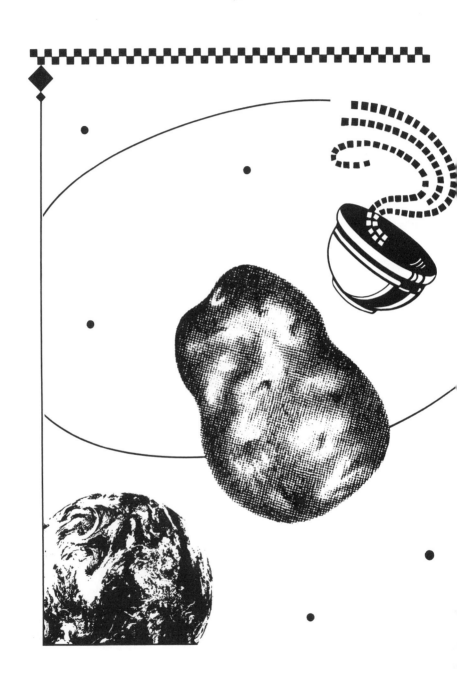

I have always wanted to be a revolutionary. I usually identify with the underdog and often advocate the overthrow of the government. I have marched in the streets. I have withheld my vote. I have quit institutions to make a point, and I automatically give preference to the alternative. And I am often very lonely.

And more often than that, utterly destitute.

And what difference does it make? What does it prove? For all the resentment and rage I feel toward this male dominated, capitalistic, nuclear family oriented,

alienating society that we live in; this sexist, racist, classist, ageist, looksist, speciesist, homophobic state of oppression that we call Amerika; I cannot bear to think of my father as a male chauvinist pig and I sometimes wish I could be close with my family.

I have almost unbearably fond recollections of family picnics at the lakefront on Sundays, when the lake was still clean and filled with swimming, diving pelicans. My dad and my Uncle Toby would get there early in the morning to claim a good spot under a tree near a picnic table, while the rest of the family went to church. Church. We'd set up aluminum lawn chairs for the adults and a long aluminum folding table for the food. And food there would be! My Great-aunt Mamie would cook a ham. My grandmother would fry the chicken. My Na-nan would bake a cake. My aunt would bring her girlfriend. The men took care of the soft drinks, the beer and the ice. And my mother would make the potato salad. It was her specialty. We would eat, swim, talk, laugh, play softball, take naps and sometimes just sit, enjoying the cool lake breeze and the pleasure of each other's company. Though, even then, I felt some vague stirrings of discontent, I believed I understood the universe and was sure of my position in it.

Now the lake is so filthy that swimming is prohibited. The pelicans have long since disappeared. My father is

dead. My aunt does not comprehend that I have not become a doctor, and cannot speak to me for more than thirty minutes without accusing me of having brain damage. I have trouble eating ham or chicken without feeling terrible pangs of guilt. I feel like an outsider to the human race. My family has become the enemy. And my mother still makes the best potato salad I've ever tasted.

So what do I do in this situation? Do I deny myself the pleasure of eating delicious potato salad because there are no Kentucky Fried Eggplants in the world? Do I live in poverty rather than employ my talents to support a system I perceive to be antagonistic and destructive? Do I sacrifice my life for my ideals? It is just this dilemma I hope to resolve with a little onion, a little celery, a little parsley, a little garlic, a little oil, a little vinegar, some hard boiled eggs and Hellmann's mayonnaise, a bit of salt, a dash of pepper, sliced dill pickles and a lot of boiled potatoes.

My mother's potato salad is spectacular. I really don't think she has a good time making it, but she loves hearing people tell her just how spectacular it is. Her secret is in her technique. She chops everything up into small unrecognizable pieces.

She starts with herself. Her whole life has been dedicated to self-sacrifice for the benefit of others. To spend

an extra hour in the kitchen is nothing.

She boils four medium sized potatoes in salted water. She lets them cool for a little while, but basically, while they're still pretty hot, she peels them and then cuts them up in a very special way. She holds each one in her hand (she'll bounce it a little bit to keep it from burning her too much) and cuts it vertically from top to bottom a little more than halfway down the potato. Then she lays it on its side, still in her hand (bouncing more carefully now; this part is pretty important), and cuts horizontally across the vertical cuts so that she gets about fifteen small rectangular potato pieces. Then she repeats the entire process on the other half of the potato in her hand, and then on yet the other three. She drops all the potato pieces in a large mixing bowl and prepares to begin her secret technique.

She chops one medium onion, three stalks of celery, one toe of garlic, four sprigs of fresh parsley and four slices of hamburger dill pickles with her hand operated food chopper. It's important that everything be chopped very small. She takes six hard boiled eggs and separates the whites from the yellows. She chops the whites — again, very fine — and mixes the yellows with olive oil and vinegar until they form sort of a paste. Then she mixes everything together with mayonnaise, salt and pepper.

After someone she loves tastes it for her and tells her just how wonderful it is, she garnishes it with parsley and puts it in the refrigerator to cool before eating. The resulting taste sensation is an equal blend of all flavors in each mouthful.

Delicious.

There is a woman I love, and lived with for two years. She made potato salad when she wanted to and had a wonderful time doing it. She'd turn on the stereo, pour herself (me, if I wanted) some apple cider, put some potatoes on to boil and call a friend on the telephone (visit with me, prop up in front of the TV or just sit out on the porch). When the potatoes were done, she'd slice them up easily, without even thinking of peeling them, with a good knife on a wooden cutting board into haphazardly bite sized pieces. She loved a particular kind of sweet pickle, and if we had some in the refrigerator, she'd slice them up too. If we didn't, she'd hop into her car, slip a tape into the tape deck and bop to the grocery store. She'd come back with the pickles and maybe some cookies, a bottle of wine and whatever else may have tickled her fancy. She'd cut up a little onion, some hard boiled eggs and mix the whole concoction together in a big wooden bowl with mayonnaise and mustard, garlic salt, pepper and maybe something else if she felt like it. We'd eat it then, or eat it later or share it with whoever

came over or throw it out if we got tired of it or just let it sit until it got old. Sometimes it would be gone in a Sunday. Sometimes we'd munch on it for a week. Sometimes I'd get a taste of potato, pickle and egg. Sometimes I'd notice the mustard. Sometimes I'd get a big chunk of garlic salted potato. Every bite was different. I never knew what to expect. We broke up. I never could believe that she ever really loved me. Those of us who have been raised on a steady diet of oppression have often been terrified by the taste of freedom.

But taste it we must.

To live a life of meaning. To find peace. To worship the earth.

To find God in ourselves.

To live our lives openly. To take ourselves seriously. To rejoice in our happiness.

To have a good job. To drive a nice car. To take a vacation. Rob a bank.

Kill a cop.

Shoot the President.

My anger seems out of proportion. Or does it?

Has there been a war? Was there a time when wimmin ruled the earth? Was a benevolent matriarchy brutally overpowered by fiendish bands of mutant men, all documents destroyed, hidden or rewritten by the victors? Or could it have been a subtle, eroding process

where men gradually took over and women grudgingly acquiesced? Have we ever had any power at all? Are the lines that clearly drawn? Has it ever been fair? Or will it always be a constant struggle for the survival of the greediest?

I want to fight the fight.

I want my rightful place.

I want my picnic back.

I envision myself and my Lesbian sisters enjoying our vegetables on the very lakefront where my family has been. Our volleyball net is our banner, firm against the breeze; our "Freaked Out Dykes On Radiation" T-shirts, our proud uniforms. We have cleaned the lake, distributed the wealth and eliminated the threat of the dreaded nuclear cloud. The work has been done. We have made the world safe. Surrounding picnickers are humbled by our courageous integrity; envious of our joy, our power, our health, our insights into the secrets of existence.

I, of course, have brought the potato salad. It has become my specialty.

But this potato salad has not been easy to come by.

I went into my backyard to pull some potatoes up out of the ground, to lovingly stroke the hens that would lay the eggs that I would hard boil, to chop the trees that would provide the wood for the coops I would build to

shelter the mother hens from marauding neighborhood felines who would terrorize the eggs that might become chicks as I pondered whether or not I should kill them. I discovered instead a nice Mexican tile patio with two quite comfortable looking lawn chairs and a patch of green shady banana trees, swaying slightly in an unseasonably warm autumn breeze. So this is what my backyard looks like, I said to myself as I considered sitting myself down, stretching myself out, enjoying the day and mentally acquiring the ingredients I would need for my dish.

Potatoes, I thought.

Potatoes are a lot like Lesbians. They're all the same and they're all different.

You have New potatoes, Russett potatoes. Red potatoes, brown potatoes. Boiled potatoes, fried potatoes. Baked potatoes, peeled potatoes. But all potatoes are composed of carbohydrates and water. They're all easily digestable. They all absorb fats well. And they all have Vitamin C in their skins.

Some of us play softball. Some of us weave missles of cloth in protest of the nuclear arms race. Some of us wear three piece suits and do our daily work in courtrooms where we defend against what we see as unjust. Some of us don't do a damn thing at all. Some of us aren't even gay. Some of us are men. Men? What am I

saying? One time I said in front of a lot of people (from a stage, actually) that men could be dykes too. I heard myself later on a tape and I wondered what in the world I could have meant. A friend of mine asked me, "Just tell me," she said, a little concerned for me it seemed, "how can a man be a dyke?" I guess partly I had a male friend in the audience and I wanted him to feel welcome. But it was more than that. Maybe I use the word "Lesbian" the way the rest of the world uses "Man," or the more enlightened, "Humankind." I've had to see myself in "Man" since I was a little girl. Now it's the world's turn to see itself in me. That's what I mean. Potatoes.

I wanted to add something with color to my plain white potatoes with red or brown skins, so I started thinking about celery — which, although a lovely pale green, is actually a member of the bright orange carrot family — and I remembered a time when my boss made a pass at me over dinner in a very fine restaurant. I told him I was gay. But what if I hadn't been gay? I could have told him I was married or engaged. But what if I weren't? I could have told him I had a boyfriend. But what if I didn't? Would it have made any difference anyway? I wonder if I could have just told him no? What if I were black? Whether or not I would have revealed my color to him would not have been the issue.

The issue here is the power dynamic. The issue here is being on the wrong end of a very unequal balance of power. The issue here is discrimination and unfairness and how to rise against it without losing the self to it. The issue here is how to keep ourselves fed.

Do you know that some people put olives in their potato salad? Have you ever heard of such a thing? I thought I'd add something a little outrageous myself.

We are here and we want wives! Where are our wives? Godammit woman, bring me my slippers!

Imagine fresh coffee every morning, hot breakfast on the table, clothes that have been laundered and mended appearing continually, as if by their own volition, in the dresser drawers. A lunch packed, a sweet kiss goodbye on the cheek. A welcoming supper when you get home. A cold beer and a soft recliner. Football game on TV. A household running according to your needs and desires. Warm, loving sex on clean sheets at night. Someone to carry your children.

Imagine working eight hours a day, five days a week — if you're lucky enough to be working at all — in a system that could possibly destroy you in order to support a mate who probably hates you.

So much for olives.

When shocked by the outrageous, dash back to the familiar! I thought I'd chop up some onions.

I considered borrowing my mom's little hand powered dime store food chopper (you know — the one she uses to pulverize eggs), but the truth is, I actually went out and bought one myself. Isn't that funny? After all the grief I gave her for using one. Sometimes I've caught myself standing at the kitchen counter, hitting and pounding, cutting up onions of all things — even weeping from them — and feeling so mad at my boss who treats me unfairly, or my mother who wronged me when I was a child, or my lover who won't give me complete and total fidelity for the rest of our lives — just banging that thing really hard and thinking that maybe my mother wasn't quite so foolish after all.

If we all chopped ourselves up really fine like my mom, and committed ourselves to a life of egalitarian sharing, we could possibly all live a modest life, maybe even a good one. But all of us won't. Goddess knows, the people in power won't willingly give up the power they have to the people who don't. Sometimes I think the only people who are willing to consider giving up power are those people who have little or no power to begin with.

And if those of us who don't have much power keep cutting ourselves up — getting ourselves thrown in jail, starving ourselves on principle, demanding adherence to strict political codes after the usefulness of them has run

its course: Lesbians rejecting straight women, gay men rejecting all women, white against black, straight against gay, women against men, people against animals — then the ruling class, the people who have so much more than they need it's obscene, will continue to serve us up for supper on finer and finer china in secluded oak paneled dining rooms, climatically controlled by nuclear powered thermostats of doom.

There won't be any picnic left to fight for at all.

Now picture a picnic dish of only potatoes.

Peel a raw onion and take a big bite of it. Clear your sinuses and burn a hole in your stomach. Chew a toe of fresh garlic and freshen your breath with a sprig of fresh parsley. You know what you can do with hard boiled eggs and Hellmann's mayonnaise, but you just had that yesterday.

I am making a point here of mutual dependency, personal integrity and the successful combination of the two.

I will not sacrifice myself because some may find my taste too pungent or my contribution insignificant. I want to be part of the salad. I deserve it. I'm in the recipe.

Let's not quibble about details. Some of us might like dill pickles. Some of us might prefer our pickles sweet. Some of us might even go for olives. Take a chance.

Open up. Though there are many different ways to make it, potato salad is always potato salad.

So I'm sitting here in the lap of my lawn chair ruminating on potatoes and joy, and struggle and strife, and I realize that I've decided to eat crackers and cheese. I've fixed myself quite an attractive plate of Stoned Wheat Thin Crackers from the Whole Food Store down the street and spread them with special herb mustard. I've cut a selection of cheeses and quartered a crisp, juicy apple. A friend of mine has come over to join me with a pitcher of iced tea, and we seem to be celebrating the two of us separate, together and alive in the world.

I wonder that the picnic I envisioned might not come to pass, any more than my father will return from the dead. But I do know that bright curly green parsley I can cut from a garden is suitable for garnishing all of our dishes.

Fruit
Drink

went to church last Sunday during a hurricane. It was the first time I'd been since my father died. Has it really been so many years? I remember we sang the hymn "Jesus Savior, Pilot Me" especially for him and I had wanted to cry, but I wouldn't. Oh, don't think I went to church because of the hurricane. I've been through many storms before; and though some have made me think strongly about buying a boat and loading it up with a dove, an olive branch and two of everything I have in the house, this one seemed not so religious. Just a lot of rain that gave no indication of

stopping and a wind that rendered umbrellas useless and raincoats only trappers of water.

I was feeling somewhat rundown — perhaps from all the swimming and biking and running I do to build up my physical strength — not to mention, a little hungover. So I drank some Knudsen's Natural Breakfast Juice, which I prayed would help heal me with, as it says on the label, its pineapple, white grape, orange, grapefruit, lemon, lime and tangerine juices from concentrates with natural citrus flavors. But I wasn't really sure that it contained all of those things and wasn't just tap water and sugar and questionable additives. I wasn't really sure I should be going to this church on the corner of Port and Burgundy Streets where I had been baptised in tiny white garments, and which has housed my family on my mother's side — though my mom has splintered off to a church nearer her neighborhood now — literally for generations. But I had simply made up my mind. Neither my feeling under the weather, nor the weather itself, nor even the woman I love lying provocatively on the sofa asking me how on earth I could leave her on this cozy so good to be inside type of morning to go of all places to church would sway me from my quest.

I pulled my dress out of the closet, thought about pantyhose, pumps and a purse, and put it right back. I have a hard enough time recognizing God; I didn't want

to make it hard for God to know me. I chose instead my favorite black I call them "Art Pants," black socks with little gray and white cats on them, my running shoes and a white heavy cotton sweater.

I wanted to run up the stone steps of my old church to the oaken double doors at the top, lifting my knees high and pushing hard off the balls of my feet. Yet I felt myself ascending one slow step at a time as if there were hands gripping the backs of my shoes. I felt small and frightened with the wind and the rain whipping around me under the darkening sky. I was afraid that the bells would start pealing, the building would begin to shudder, crack and crumble, and the steeple would topple, the cross at the peak of it plunging deep into my bosom. I imagined that Jesus His Very Self might step down from the huge mural I remembered encircling the altar where He stands with His pierced hands outstretched, surrounded by angels, humbled parishioners and sheep, His flaming forefinger pointed at me, His celestial voice thundering, "Unclean! Unclean!"

I stepped in. It was early. The church was quiet, almost empty. I shook off a storm that seemed impotent now that I was inside this strong, sturdy building. A man with white hair gave me a bulletin and smiled. I saw a cardboard box decorated with wrapping paper with a slot cut out in the top of it to collect donations for the

victims of the earthquake in Mexico. The mural was much smaller than I had remembered. I walked down the aisle, picked a pew not too far to the front, not too far to the back, to the right and sat down. I felt like I wanted to cry, but I didn't.

I felt isolated and different from the arriving husband and wife couples, the sometimes pious sometimes scampering children, the elderly ladies in their matching hats and gloves. I suddenly wanted to jump up and run, a heathen escaping her captors, until I looked up and saw someone who looked just like me. It was my aunt — my mother's younger sister. She and I have almost exactly the same face.

My aunt never married, but she's lived with the same woman since college. She assures me that they are not gay. My aunt and her womanfriend are of different faiths, so my aunt worships alone today as do I. She doesn't see me, yet walks to the very pew in which I am sitting. She stands to pray for a moment, resting her age spotted hands on her umbrella as if it were a cane. My God, she's in her seventies now! She was in her seventies the last time I saw her, but somehow I seem to ignore it. I still tend to see her as that striking athletic woman who wore pants and never brought food to our family picnics. I believe she is delighted when she sees me and I move over to be with her.

"Do you always sit here?" I ask her.

"Yes," she answers me. "Carol and Billy (my cousin and her husband) might be coming with Eric (their son), but I don't know, with this weather. I know your Nanan's still sick. And Toby (my godfather) probably came to early church. But yes," she tells me again, this time lifting an eyebrow as she looks at me, "this is where we all sit."

Before I can marvel at what homing instinct has guided me to this very pew, the music of the organ is swirling about the church air, cracking its stillness with jubilance. A procession of singers in bright purple robes, ministers in white — why aren't any of them women? — and altar boys — not girls, even yet? — carrying aloft a shimmering metal cross has swept forth from the rear of the church. Like a sharp gust of wind, we are all up and singing.

"A mighty fortress is our God, a trusty shield and weapon."

I worry about how many witches have been burned at the stake, the flaming faggots at their feet ignited by Christians, yet my voice wants to rise for the sheer joy of singing along with the rest. Of course the key is not right for me — probably perfect for the damn men — so where I want to be strong, I must either force out a very low bass or sing very high. I am timid at first; but as I

hear my aunt unfaltering beside me, I become bolder.

"The kingdom ours remaineth!" we sing in falsetto together.

We sit down and stand up and sit down and stand up again. The minister says, "Amen," and we say "Hallelujah," and he says "Hallelujah," and we say, "Amen." Every now and then we sing songs. It doesn't much matter. What matters is that everyone is here week after week, year after year, generation after generation trying to hold on to the same thing.

Like me in the bar on Saturday night.

When the minister begins his sermon, I know it's going to be about homosexuals burning in Hell and I'm frightened. Not about burning in Hell. I'm afraid that I'll have to stand up in front of God and everybody and say, "This is wrong. You wouldn't say Black people were going to burn in Hell if there were any out here in the congregation, now would you, even if you truly believed it? You might say, 'Get those Negroes out of here.' But I don't think you would just gloss over them like they didn't exist. So I want you to know, at least, that I am here and you're talking to me."

But what does this minister say? He says, "The topic of today's sermon is Freedom from Oppression."

Can you beat that?

I sat back ready to be challenged, enlightened or even

enraged. I found myself lulled and confused. I noticed that I was scrutinizing the paint job on the ceiling, planning what I was going to do at work on Monday, trying to decide whether or not I should blow my nose in church. Just moments after the little girl sitting next to me started quietly singing Donna Summer songs to her doll, the minister granted us peace. Then we all began singing again and plates were passed out for money and cards that had been filled out by people who wanted to take communion.

The music deepened to a somber minor key. The minister ceremoniously held up wafers of Jesus and shot glasses of His blood given into death for my sins. This is the meat of it, I thought. Walking through fire. Handling snakes. Eating flesh.

I found myself waiting in line to kneel at the altar.

Maybe people like me are like Jesus, I thought, my knees on the carpet, my head bowed, my hands folded on the railing in front of me. We are people with burdens to carry, people who suffer abuse, people on whom anger is unleashed simply because we are who we happen to be. But we take it because we're stronger and maybe other people can't. We take it for them, for the earth, to help solve the problems. We absorb the evil of people who hate, to keep them from destroying everything else. Sometimes we hurt and some of us die, but

that's just the way it has been. And then I thought that maybe that's what Jesus did when She died on the cross. That maybe that's what She continues to do every time She gives Her body for us to eat and Her blood for us to drink and I raised my head to receive Her.

This is my body.

No, the wafer did not sear a smoldering cross into the roof of my mouth. But the sweet blood red wine was in fact hot as it washed over my tongue and burned its way down my throat. It was as hot as that beautiful woman who had led an adoring procession of worshipers back and forth across a dance floor throbbing with music just the night before at the bar.

Can I buy you a drink?

I had been sitting on a stool with a glass of wine in my hand. "She looks familiar," I told a friend of mine who had friends of her own on the lookout to tell her when the woman would be passing by again so she could just look. She was that beautiful.

"Sure she looks familiar," she shouted to me over the music. "Probably from the cover of a magazine."

I pressed my fingertips lightly over my own face with its nose too big, cheeks too full. Sometimes I feel very sad that I am who I am and not someone for whom doors are opened more easily. Sometimes I feel bitter and angry that my life so far has not been such an easy

one, and I wish for someone or something beyond me. Could I be wishing for the face of God? Could it be She with Whom I seek to commune week after week in the bar drinking wine with my friends?

Still the wine warms my belly as I kneel here at the altar with strangers who might hate or condemn me if they knew who I was yet I feel a sudden peace which passeth all understanding and I know that if there is not forgiveness around me, there is forgiveness within me. But how do I know that this feeling is God and not just a quick rush of sugar and alcohol from a fermented grape?

My aunt and I hugged goodbye in the parking lot outside of the church, letting ourselves be drenched together for a moment in the rain. I felt my muscles and bones beginning to ache. Our spirits filled with peace and acceptance, were we exposing our bodies for just a moment too long to a wrath of God pouring on Earth? Or was it only pouring on me standing outside of an umbrella of faith?

Now the storm is over, and here I am sick. My head is congested and it hurts and throbs if I bend down even just a little. My limbs are getting weaker and weaker. My nose is stopped up and I can hardly breathe. My skin feels hot. I'm getting cranky. I am cranky.

I'm not giving in.

I get on my bike. I lock my feet into the toe clips that are bolted to the pedals. I pull up with one leg and push down with the other. I slice through the air moving faster and faster. I stand up and push and pull harder. I come to an overpass. I take it on still standing up. My thighs begin to burn. My breathing is stabbing my chest. I make it to the top. I shift into my most efficient gear and, descending effortlessly, realize that I am almost flying, pushing into a wind that, I see more and more clearly, is not blowing from a storm outside of myself. As I hit the straightaway, each push and pull motion takes me further than I would have thought possible. I turn around and do it again.

I go to the pool. The water is colder than I would have liked. I'm still feeling miserably sick, but my body itself is growing stronger and stronger. I lift my left elbow, bring it up over my head, drop my hand, slightly cupped, fingers first into the water and stroke. I stroke again with my right arm, then my left arm, then my right, then I turn my head to the side while my left elbow is still in the air and I breathe. I kick, my legs held out straight, toes pointed, one two three kicks to each stroke. I follow the black line on the bottom of the pool back and forth until I realize that I'm breathing on every stroke and it still doesn't seem like enough air. I seem to be getting a chill. I give up and go into the sauna to

sweat. To sweat out whatever evil is destroying me. And in one weakened moment, though my nakedness seems to be taking on a surprisingly somewhat beautiful form that I would never have thought could be mine, I'm afraid that everything I've been told is wrong with me is true. That I, in fact, was not welcome in God's house.

I decide to go home to my own house.

I think my lover and I should have sex.

Could she instead, she wants to know, fix me some hot apple cider sprinkled with fresh allspice, cloves, pieces of orange peel and cinnamon sticks in a thick ceramic mug?

No, it would be better if we had sex.

Could she, she asks me again, simply cradle me in the crook of her arm, hold the steaming mug to my lips and let its sweet liquid trickle gently down my throat?

I still think that we should have sex. But I reluctantly yield to her arms, her fruit drink and the dreamlike invitation of slumber. My head gives an involuntary jerk. My eyes open wide to click a final photograph of all that is around me. It blurs to but a pinhole of light and I am gone.

As quickly as that, I'm awake.

It is the moonlight on my face — or is it the dawn? No, what has wakened me is the sudden cessation of suffering. My breathing is no longer ragged. My head is

clear and light. My muscles are vibrant with an energy I had believed was beyond me. My body and the body of this woman who loves me seem to be absorbing what brightness there is. We appear to be glowing with a light that could be coming from paradise. I could easily pull her to me, kneel before her and greedily drink from her persimmon lips now parted in open invitation. I lightly touch her sleeping face instead. Or is it my own that I stroke?

For breakfast, I mix in a blender a drink of fresh strawberries, an almost overripe banana, crushed ice and the juice of an orange that I squeeze myself in my U.S. Patented hand powered Juice-O-Mat, bought for 50¢ at a Lutheran Thrift Store where my mom sent me one time when I needed a sofa; and I drink it purely for the taste of it.

Could it really be so simple?

Of course not.

But in this moment, it is and I am.

I open my door to the brightness of this particular day, and I know that through it I will run well. I will run through hectic daily life and through peaceful fruit orchards and groves. I will run to Port and Burgundy and to simple red wine at the bar. I will run back and forth through sickness and storms into health and sunlight as naturally as a pendulum swings from one side to the

other. I will run with strangers. I will run with my father, my aunt, my mother, my lover, the beautiful young woman on the dance floor. I will run with people who won't want to be running with me. I will enter a race. If I finish fiftieth, who will be forty-ninth? If I finish twelfth, who will be eleventh? If I finish first, who will be ahead of me? I stand on the threshold balanced on one leg, the other pulled behind me in a stretch. I find myself looking ahead, but I know that I'm already there.

The Crossing Press Feminist Series includes the following titles:

Abeng, A Novel by Michelle Cliff

Clenched Fists, Burning Crosses, A Novel by Chris South

Crystal Visions, Nine Meditations for Personal and Planetary Peace by Diane Mariechild

Feminist Spirituality and the Feminine Divine, An Annotated Bibliography by Anne Carson

Folly, A Novel by Maureen Brady

Learning Our Way: Essays in Feminist Education, edited by Charlotte Bunch and Sandra Pollack

Lesbian Etiquette, Humorous Essays by Gail Sausser

Lesbian Images, Literary Commentary by Jane Rule

Magic Mommas, Trembling Sisters, Puritans & Perverts, Feminist Essays by Joanna Russ

Mother, Sister, Daughter, Lover, Stories by Jan Clausen

Mother Wit: A Feminist Guide to Psychic Development by Diane Mariechild

Movement, A Novel by Valerie Miner

Movement in Black, Poetry by Pat Parker

Natural Birth, Poetry by Toi Derricotte

Nice Jewish Girls: A Lesbian Anthology, edited by Evelyn Torton Beck

The Notebooks of Leni Clare and Other Short Stories by Sandy Boucher

The Politics of Reality: Essays in Feminist Theory by Marilyn Frye

On Strike Against God, A Lesbian Love Story by Joanna Russ

The Queen of Wands, Poetry by Judy Grahn

Red Beans & Rice, Recipes for Lesbian Health and Wisdom by Bode Noonan

Sinking, Stealing, A Novel by Jan Clausen

Sister Outsider, Essays and Speeches by Audre Lorde

Winter's Edge, A Novel by Valerie Miner

Women Brave in the Face of Danger, Photographs of Latin and North American Women by Margaret Randall

The Work of A Common Woman, Poetry by Judy Grahn

Zami: A New Spelling of My Name, Biomythography by Audre Lorde